Get Wed for Less

Some related titles from How To Books

Wedding Speeches for Women
The girls' own guide to giving a speech they'll remember

The Complete Best Man
How to turn a terrifying prospect into a piece of cake

How to Make a Great Wedding Speech
A practical, comprehensive, entertaining and effective book for anyone who has to make a wedding speech

Making the Father of the Bride's Speech

howtobooks
Practical books that inspire

Please send for a free copy of the latest catalogue to:
How To Books
Spring Hill House, Spring Hill Road, Begbroke,
Oxford OX5 1RX, United Kingdom
info@howtobooks.co.uk
www.howtobooks.co.uk

Get Wed for Less

for Less

A Bride's Guide

Elizabeth Catherine Myers

howtobooks

Published by How To Books Ltd,
Spring Hill House, Spring Hill Road,
Begbroke, Oxford OX5 1RX, United Kingdom
Tel: (01865) 375794. Fax: (01865) 379162
email: info@howtobooks.co.uk
www.howtobooks.co.uk

British Library Cataloguing in Publication Data
A catalogue record for this book is available from the
British Library

ISBN 978 1 84528 210 3

Cartoons by Phill Burrows
Cover design by Baseline Arts Ltd, Oxford
Produced for How To Books by Deer Park Productions, Tavistock
Typeset by Pantek Arts Ltd, Maidstone, Kent.
Printed and bound by Cromwell Press, Trowbridge, Wiltshire

Contents

Contents

Dedication

A BIG thank you to

My mum and dad
for encouraging me to never give up

Andrew
for always being on my side

Rachel
for your assistance and cheerful nature

And to Jonathan
for making me the happiest person alive when you asked me to
marry you.

The checklists provided under each section are reproduced, larger, at the end of the book and are aimed to be used by you. They have been designed so you can photocopy them and take them with you when you go to venues or meet with suppliers.

Preface

If you mention the word 'wedding', what are the things that spring to mind?

- romance

- special day

- happiness

- beautiful dress

- flowers

- bridesmaids

- church.

However, when it comes down to actually planning the event, it can be very stressful. Cost and budget are two key areas to think about. Decisions about where to hold the wedding and reception are important as well as who to invite. In addition, coping with family members and trying to balance making them happy without letting them take control of your wedding can make it even more difficult.

Although I can't offer assistance with resolving family issues, this guidebook aims to break down the different areas of organising a wedding reception. I have provided checklists for each area as well as tips on how to save money.

I have worked in event management for several years and been involved in organising many large scale conferences and formal dinners. Using the skills I acquired, I launched a wedding planning service providing low cost wedding packages for couples in the Leicestershire area.

I have spent over 18 months researching the concept for the service and therefore gained vast amounts of information which has now been condensed into this guidebook.

Introduction

Congratulations!

You've decided to get engaged. You've shared the happy news with your families and friends. You are feeling on top of the world.

You then start planning your wedding day...

You begin to spend all your weekends at wedding fairs.

Venues are booked up months or years in advance.

The guest list starts to grow.

You are faced with different menus and different pricing structures which are impossible to compare.

The minute you mention the word wedding the price of everything seems to double.

The endless choices of colour schemes/wedding cars/photographers/cakes/entertainers make you feel dizzy.

You are surrounded by piles and piles of brochures and leaflets which confuse you further.

The costs start spiralling out of control.

'How am I going to get through this?' you think to yourself...

Put the kettle on or pour yourself a drink, put your feet up and read on to find out how to plan your wedding reception whilst at the same time saving you hundreds (and possibly thousands) of pounds.

Too Good to be True?

If you have already done some research into your wedding reception you may wonder whether it is possible to save money and still hold a wedding reception to be proud of.

Over 18 months of research has gone into this manual to find cost cutting solutions for your wedding day.

However, in order to save money you are likely to need the following.

Time

A lot of the costs involved in a wedding reception are for labour — whether it's the time involved in making hand-made invitations or the time involved in making the cake. If you can do some of these tasks yourself, you will already begin to save money.

Effort

The solutions to finding ways to cut the cost of your wedding reception may not always be easy to find. You may need to spend considerable effort and time in contacting many different suppliers to get the best deal. Negotiation is also important.

Vision

You need to spend some time picturing how you would like your wedding day to look. You also need to decide what is essential to make your wedding day complete. Once you have a vision in your mind, it is far easier to make a start on sourcing the services/items that you need to make the vision reality.

Family and friends

Now is the time to call upon your family and friends. You've heard the saying 'many hands make light work'. These people could help you with both time and effort and their ideas could help you with vision. Furthermore, if they have a particular talent, e.g. photography, DJ-ing or playing in a band, perhaps they could give their services, at a reduced rate, free of charge or as your wedding present.

However, if you go for this option you need to ensure they are happy to take on the responsibility of their task and will be 100% reliable on the day.

Where can I save money?

1 Hen/stag/hag party

2 Venue

3 Catering

4 Wedding cake

5 Car and chauffeur

6 Photographer

7 Invitations

8 Decorations

9 Flowers

10 DJ and disco/entertainment

11 Wedding dress and other clothing

12 Task list for planning your wedding day

The checklists provided under each section are aimed to be used by you and have been designed so you can photocopy them and take them with you when you go to venues or meet with suppliers.

1 The Hen or Stag Party

One of the traditions associated with getting married is the celebration of 'one last night of freedom' through holding a stag party for the groom and a hen party for the bride.

As these are separate events both of which need planning and organising, it would be possible to write a separate guidebook just on this section. However, as organising the stag and hen parties is in the checklist at the back of this guidebook, I thought it was necessary to include a short section on this topic.

Remember that the organisation of the stag and hen parties is usually the responsibility of the best man and chief bridesmaid, so perhaps this section of the book should be passed on to them to get them started, with ideas on what to organise and where to begin.

In most cases the stags and hens all pay for themselves for the stag or hen party, therefore it is important to find out early on what amount everyone can afford.

It has also recently become fashionable to combine hen and stag nights into a joint hag night. This is likely to have an impact on what you decide to do so the evening can cater for all tastes.

Questions for the organisers

	Stag	Hen
What is the budget per person for the stag/hen night?	£_____	£_____
What is the location for the stag/hen night?	At home ☐ Local ☐ Other city ☐ Outside UK ☐	At home ☐ Local ☐ Other city ☐ Outside UK ☐

The Hen or Stag Party

What activities will you want to take part in on the stag/hen night?

Watching football ☐
Gokarting ☐
Paintballing ☐
Pub crawl ☐
Meal out ☐
Nightclub ☐
Karaoke ☐
Other ☐

_____
_____
_____

Spa/beauty ☐
Pub crawl ☐
Meal out ☐
Nightclub ☐
Karaoke ☐
Other ☐

_____
_____
_____

What are the costs per person?

Activity £_____
Drinks £_____
Food £_____
Nightclub entrance
£_____
Transport £_____
Accommodation
£_____
Clothing
e.g. printed t-shirts
£_____
Other £_____

Activity £_____
Drinks £_____
Food £_____
Nightclub entrance
£_____
Transport £_____
Accommodation
£_____
Clothing
e.g. printed t-shirts
£_____
Other £_____

(!) Cost cutting tips and ideas

The costs for a hen/stag party can soon add up when you start to take food, alcohol, accommodation, transport and any other leisure activities into account. With the introduction of low-cost flights it has become easier for people to hold hen and stag weekends in European cities with the bill running into hundreds of pounds per person.

At a time when the bride and groom are already spending money on their wedding day, some careful planning and a bit of creativity can result in hen and stag nights which are unforgettable, but do not cost a fortune at a time when funds are likely to be stretched.

- Think local – going to another city or abroad involves transport costs and possibly overnight accommodation. If you choose to do something nearer to home, it will save cash. If your friends live locally it won't break the bank for them too.

- Rather than going out, think about a stag/hen/hag (a combined hen and stag party) party at home. If your guests all bring a bottle, there shouldn't be too many other costs involved. There is still a lot of scope to be creative with party games and fancy dress to make it the most talked about event (until your wedding reception!).

- Keep it low-key and sophisticated. You might feel that a large stag or hen party is not for you. Perhaps celebrating with a couple of close friends or family members sounds more appealing.

- Without wanting to sound negative, another option is to decide whether you actually want a hen or stag party at all. In particular for the stags, we have all heard of many horror stories of grooms waking up at the opposite end of the country or finding themselves chained naked to a lamp post! Of course, a stag or hen party is a great way to get together with all your friends before your wedding day, but it may be worth thinking carefully about whether *YOU* actually want to take part in the activities of your stag or hen night, or do you feel you ought to due to the pressure from your friends?

2 Venue

Venue for the Wedding Ceremony

One of the first decisions you will need to make about your wedding is where to have the actual wedding ceremony.

If you are having a civil ceremony it must be conducted at a Register Office or at a venue which holds a licence for civil ceremonies.

If you choose to get married at a Register Office you should contact the staff there, who will advise you on the procedure of booking the correct date and time for your wedding. They will also advise you on all the formalities associated with giving notice of your intention to marry, the documents you will need to produce, the fees you will need to pay and the necessary timescale to allow.

If you choose to get married at a venue approved for civil marriages, you should contact the venue to make a reservation and staff there will advise you on which Register Office to contact regarding the legal formalities.

If you are having a Church of England or Church in Wales wedding ceremony, you will need to contact the parish minister/vicar of the church you want to get married in. They will advise you on steps you need to take to ensure you can get married on the day you have chosen and comply with marriage legalities.

Scotland has its owns laws regarding marriage, so if you are proposing to get married in Scotland contact the venue for advice on what steps you need to take.

For a marriage ceremony in a religious building (e.g. a church [other than the Church of England], a mosque or a temple), you should contact the religious leader for advice on the correct procedures you should follow.

If in doubt, contact the venue where you want to get married and ask for advice on what you need to do. Venues that are licensed for wedding ceremonies will be used to advising couples.

You will probably need to start looking for a reception venue at the same time as you start to make arrangements for your wedding ceremony. Until you have confirmation that your wedding ceremony can take place on the date and at the time you propose, keep the venue booking as provisional, but keep in touch with the venue to let them know how you are getting on with arrangements and when you will be able to confirm the booking.

Searching for your reception venue will probably be the most time con-suming task you face. First of all it is important to clarify what you are looking for in a venue.

(?) Questions for the bride and groom

How many guests are
you hoping to invite?   _____

What type of venue   Traditional ☐   Modern ☐   Other ☐
are you looking for?

What type of   City/town ☐   Countryside ☐   Other ☐
location are you
looking for?

How far are you and   _____ miles
your guests willing
to travel from the
wedding ceremony
venue to the
wedding reception
venue?

Do you want outside caterers or a venue that supplies the catering?	Outside caterers ☐	Internal Catering ☐
Which day of the week would you like to hold your reception on?	_____	
What time do you want the day reception to start/finish?	Start:	Finish:
What time do you want the evening reception to start/finish?	Start:	Finish:
Do you want overnight accommodation for your guests on site?	Yes ☐	No ☐
Do you want the venue to have a licensed bar?	Yes ☐	No ☐
Are you looking for a venue where you can have a sit down meal?	Yes ☐	No ☐

Are you looking for   Yes ☐   No ☐
somewhere suitable
for a finger buffet?

Why the Expense?

Your venue and food are probably going to be the biggest expense of your wedding day.

Remember, if you are hoping to save money, you are going to have to be creative with your venue search.

The venues which are already popular for holding wedding receptions are likely to charge higher prices. If they get plenty of bookings for wedding receptions, they are unlikely to negotiate on price as they know they can fill the venue at the set prices they already charge.

Summer Saturdays will be days of peak demand for wedding reception venues and therefore the more popular places need to make good levels of profit on these days. (If you decide to hold your wedding reception during the week, it may be possible to negotiate cheaper prices.)

Venues that hold wedding fairs or advertise prominently in local wedding magazines are probably not the best ones to approach if you are trying to cut costs.

Where Should I Look?

When I was setting up my wedding planning service I spent 12 months searching for venues and visited over 150 venues in the Leicestershire area. There was a huge range in terms of size, appearance and location.

I found the following searching techniques the most helpful.

Internet

Searching for function rooms on the internet was a useful starting place. It provided telephone numbers for several venues, but on the whole there was not much detail about the function rooms on websites so telephone contact was necessary, followed up by a visit in person to see each venue.

Directories

Local telephone directories were another good source of contact telephone numbers for various venues.

Local press

Some venues take out small adverts in the local press so it is always worth keeping a look out for these as and when they appear.

On foot or by car

Once you have selected a location that appeals to you it may be worth driving or walking around that area to see if you come across any undis-covered venues.

Word of mouth

Talk to everyone you know about your wedding reception and ask people for suggestions. Try family members, friends, friends of friends, work colleagues or anyone you bump into when you are out and about. Most people will have attended a wedding reception, party or function in recent months and may be able to point you in the direction of a venue you never knew about.

The next few pages will give you some ideas of the different types of venues you might want to consider for holding your wedding reception.

Smaller Hotels/Guest Houses/Restaurants/Bars/Pub Function Rooms

In my experience these types of venue can lend themselves well to a wedding reception. Most should offer in-house catering which makes things easier from an organisational point of view.

 **Questions to ask the venue**

Can the venue accommodate the number of guests?   Yes ☐   No ☐

Is there a separate room or area to hold the reception away from other customers?   Yes ☐   No ☐

Can the hotel or guest house restaurant area be converted into a private function room?

Yes ☐   No ☐

Can we use the dining area for our reception on the day of the week we are proposing to hold it?

Yes ☐   No ☐

What options are available for food?

Hot sit down waiter service ☐
Hot fork buffet ☐
Cold fork buffet ☐
Finger buffet ☐
Barbecue ☐
Other ☐

Is there a licensed bar available?

Yes ☐   No ☐

What time are last orders?

_____

Is it possible to get a bar extension?

Yes ☐   No ☐

If yes, is there an extra cost for this?

Yes ☐ £_____   No ☐

Venue

Is it possible for us to bring wine/sparkling wine/champagne?

Yes ☐　　　　　　No ☐

Is there a corkage fee associated with this?

Wine　　　　　£_____
Sparkling wine　£_____
Champagne　　£_____

Will the venue supply glasses if we bring our own wine/champagne?

Yes ☐　　　　　　No ☐

Will there be an additional cost for this?

Yes ☐ £_____　　No ☐

Is the venue child friendly?

Yes ☐　　　　　　No ☐

Are the toilets in good working order?

Yes ☐　　　　　　No ☐

Are there enough?

Yes ☐　　　　　　No ☐

Is there enough parking?

Yes ☐　　　　　　No ☐

Is there accommodation available on site for guests?

Yes ☐　　　　　　No ☐

If yes, what would be the cost per night?

£_____

Is it possible to get a discounted rate if the reception is held at the venue?

Yes ☐   No ☐

If no, where is the nearest accommodation for guests?

_____

_____

_____

Is it possible to have a disco for the evening reception?

Yes ☐   No ☐

Are there any restrictions regarding this such as noise or space?

Yes ☐   No ☐

Always check with the venue manager about public liability insurance, certificates of food hygiene (for in-house catering) and licensing issues regarding the sale of alcohol and entertainment. Ask to see certificates.

Community Centres/Sport Clubhouses/Social Clubs/ College Halls

Another alternative I found is to hire a hall for a relatively low price. However, you need to remember that you may have to organise assistance with moving furniture, setting the hall up as well as cleaning the hall and putting the furniture away afterwards. Unless you have an army of willing friends to do this, you might end up paying for cleaners etc., which might not make the cost saving for the hall worthwhile.

In addition, these types of venue are unlikely to have in-house catering and therefore this will be another separate item to organise.

(?) Questions to ask the venue

Is the hall in a suitable condition to hold a wedding reception? Yes ☐ No ☐

Is the hall suitable and clean enough to serve food? Yes ☐ No ☐

Is the hall available for hire on the day of the week we are proposing to hold it? Yes ☐ No ☐

Will the hall provide:

tables Yes ☐ No ☐

chairs Yes ☐ No ☐

linen Yes ☐ No ☐

crockery Yes ☐ No ☐

cutlery Yes ☐ No ☐

glasses? Yes ☐ No ☐

What cooking and cleaning facilities are available? _____
_____
_____

Are there any caterers associated with the hall?   Yes ☐   No ☐

Is there a licensed bar available?   Yes ☐   No ☐

What time are last orders?   _____

Is it possible to get a bar extension?   Yes ☐   No ☐

If yes, is there an extra cost for this?   Yes ☐ £_____   No ☐

Is it possible for us to bring wine/sparkling wine/champagne?   Yes ☐   No ☐

Is there a corkage fee associated with this?

Wine   £_____
Sparkling wine £_____
Champagne   £_____

Will the venue supply glasses if we bring our own wine/champagne?   Yes ☐   No ☐

Will there be an additional cost for this?   Yes ☐   No ☐

Is the venue child friendly?   Yes ☐   No ☐

Will the hall be heated?   Yes ☐   No ☐

Venue

Can the hall accommodate the number of guests?	Yes ☐	No ☐
Are the toilets in good working order?	Yes ☐	No ☐
Are there enough?	Yes ☐	No ☐
Is there enough parking?	Yes ☐	No ☐
Is there accommodation available on site for guests?	Yes ☐	No ☐
If yes, what would be the cost per night?	£_____	
Is it possible to get a discounted rate if the reception is held at the venue?	Yes ☐	No ☐
If no, where is the nearest accommodation for guests?	_____ _____ _____	
When can access be gained to the hall to prepare for the reception?	_____	
When does the hall have to be vacated?	_____	

Who is responsible for cleaning and tidying the hall?	_____	

Will the hall provide staff for:

the bar	Yes ☐	No ☐
the cloakroom	Yes ☐	No ☐
moving tables and furniture?	Yes ☐	No ☐

Is it possible to have a disco for the evening reception?	Yes ☐	No ☐
Are there any restrictions regarding this such as noise?	Yes ☐	No ☐

If a venue allows you to bring your own drinks, but is unable to supply glassware, it may be possible for the caterers to supply this and also assist with pouring and serving of drinks for your guests.

Always check with the hall manager about public liability insurance and licensing issues regarding the sale of alcohol and entertainment. Ask to see certificates.

(!) Cost cutting tips and ideas

I have now given you ideas of where to look and what to ask when you find venues, but in reality what can you do to save money?

Venue

It all depends on what you are looking for on your wedding day and also the type of food you are hoping to serve your guests. I will be covering catering in the next chapter, but as this greatly affects the type of venue you will be able to choose I need to mention this now.

A traditional format for a wedding reception involves a sit-down meal after the wedding ceremony (the wedding breakfast) followed by a break for people to have a rest then by an evening reception with finger buffet and entertainment.

However, these days the format can vary from traditional to something that suits your lifestyle or reflects your individuality.

Based on my experiences of weddings I have been involved in organising, here are some of the options available which could save you hundreds of pounds.

- One couple invited a small number of close friends and family for a sit-down meal at a modern restaurant after the wedding ceremony. They then hired a local hall and had a finger buffet for a larger number of guests in the evening. By reducing numbers at the day reception, they saved money and also had a greater choice of venues that could accommodate their guests. They paid a hire fee for the hall for the evening only and managed to find caterers to supply a finger buffet at a very reasonable price.

- Another couple held their reception at a country pub which had a function room. The function room opened out onto a terrace where guests could also sit. The reception was held in the early evening and the pub manager supplied a lavish barbecue with a large range of salads. As the couple only had to feed their guests once during the day (rather than having a meal in the early afternoon and further food in the evening) they managed to save a considerable sum of money. The pub gave them the venue hire for free as they had used their in-house catering rather than bringing in their own caterers.

- A variation on this suggestion was a couple who also began their reception in the late afternoon, but decided to supply a finger buffet for their guests throughout the evening. They hired a function hall in a hotel and kept the invitation open to their guests to come and go as they pleased, but ensured the finger buffet was replenished at several times during the evening. Although they had in the region of 150-200 guests overall, this option worked out as far more economical than trying to organise a sit-down meal, but also ensured the guests were all fed adequately.

- Another option which was chosen by some friends of mine was to have a cold fork buffet for all their guests (around 100) during the afternoon. The reception finished in the early evening and people were free to go and enjoy their Saturday night in whichever way they wanted to.

The amount you can save is largely affected by the number of guests you want to invite and the type of food you would like to provide. This is covered in more detail in the next chapter.

3 Catering

As I have already mentioned, the food at your reception combined with the venue will probably be the biggest expense you will have to cover. But if you are careful about what you choose to serve your guests, it is still possible to feed everyone without bankrupting yourselves in the process.

At the same time you are clarifying what you want in terms of your venue, you also need to work out what type of food you want to serve and at what times. The venue and the food need to be compatible.

(?) Questions for the bride and groom

What type of food are you hoping to serve at your day time reception?	Hot sit down waiter service	☐
	Hot fork buffet	☐
	Cold fork buffet	☐
	Finger buffet	☐
	Barbecue	☐
	Other	☐
What type of food are you hoping to serve at your evening reception?	Hot sit down waiter service	☐
	Hot fork buffet	☐
	Cold fork buffet	☐
	Finger buffet	☐
	Barbecue	☐
	Other	☐

Is the venue compatible with the type of food you want to provide for your guests?   Yes ☐   No ☐

Does the venue have in-house caterers or is it necessary to book outside caterers?   In-house caterers ☐   Outside caterers ☐

Why the expense?

You aren't usually responsible for feeding (and paying for) so many guests and the bill for this can come as quite a shock.

As food is usually charged per head, your final bill will be directly proportional to the number of people you invite. However, if you can't cut your guest list, the alternative option is to carefully consider what you actually give your guests to eat and the times at which you feed them.

Depending on what you actually book, you need to remember that the venue/caterer has to prepare the food, possibly provide table linen/crockery, employ staff to serve and clear up often at anti-social hours, which all adds up.

What are my options?

If a venue is able to supply catering in-house, they are unlikely to allow outside caterers in. In certain circumstances they will, for example if food must be prepared in a certain way for religious reasons. However, the venue may charge a fee for using their kitchen facilities so this may work out more expensive.

In-house Catering

(?) Questions for the in-house catering manager

What type of food can you provide?

And at what prices?

Hot sit down waiter service	£_____
Hot fork buffet	£_____
Cold fork buffet	£_____
Finger buffet	£_____
Barbecue	£_____
Other	£_____

Can you give us some menus to show what type of food you can supply?　Yes ☐　　　　No ☐

Are the following items included in the price:

table linen　Yes ☐　　　　No ☐
crockery　Yes ☐　　　　No ☐
cutlery?　Yes ☐　　　　No ☐

Can you supply vegetarian options?　Yes ☐　　　　No ☐

Can you supply separate meals for people with specific dietary requirements?　Yes ☐　　　　No ☐

Is it cheaper to choose a set menu for my guests?　Yes ☐　　　　No ☐

If we set a budget per head, can you provide a menu option for that price?　Yes ☐　　　　No ☐

Is it possible to come and see a function you are providing the catering for?　Yes ☐　　　　No ☐

Always check with the venue manager about public liability insurance and certificates of food hygiene. Ask to see certificates.

Outside External Catering

If you are going to engage the services of outside caterers, it may be a good idea to ask at the venue whether there are any businesses that have provided catering at the venue before. If a caterer regularly supplies a venue, they are more likely to be familiar with the facilities and have greater knowledge of what is available on site so that they can ensure they bring any necessary equipment with them.

They may also be used to providing table linen suitable for the furniture at the venue.

Always check with the venue manager whether they will allow you to use outside/external caterers.

 **Questions for the external caterer**

What type of food can you provide?	Hot sit down waiter service	£_____
	Hot fork buffet	£_____
And at what prices?	Cold fork buffet	£_____
	Finger buffet	£_____
	Barbecue	£_____
	Other	£_____
Can you give us some menus to show what type of food you can supply?	Yes ☐	No ☐

Are the following items
included in the price:

table linen	Yes ☐	No ☐
crockery	Yes ☐	No ☐
cutlery	Yes ☐	No ☐
waitressing staff	Yes ☐	No ☐
staff to clear up?	Yes ☐	No ☐

Can you supply   Yes ☐   No ☐
vegetarian options?

Can you supply separate   Yes ☐   No ☐
meals for people with
specific dietary
requirements?

Is it cheaper to choose a   Yes ☐   No ☐
set menu for my guests?

If we set a budget per   Yes ☐   No ☐
head, can you provide a
menu option for that
price?

Do you clean up after   Yes ☐   No ☐
the function?

Is it possible to come   Yes ☐   No ☐
and see a function you
are providing the
catering for?

Have you catered at this venue before?   Yes ☐   No ☐

Will you be willing to visit the venue with us beforehand to check the facilities are suitable for the type of catering we require?   Yes ☐   No ☐

What is your contingency plan if something goes wrong beyond your control, e.g. van breakdown?   _____

If a venue allows you to bring your own drinks, but is unable to supply glassware, it may be possible for the caterers to supply this and also assist with pouring and serving of drinks for your guests. You will need to check if there is a cost attached to this.

Always check with the caterers about public liability insurance and certificates of food hygiene. Ask to see certificates.

(!) Cost cutting tips and ideas

So now you have looked at different types of venue and have considered in-house or external catering options.

Apart from cutting down the guest list, where is it possible to make savings without compromising quality or losing your guests to the local take-away?

Based on my past experience of many different types of wedding reception, here are a few ideas that other people have used in the past.

- If you are going to have a sit-down reception during the day, it is possible to reduce the cost by choosing a cold fork buffet rather than a hot sit down meal. Cold food tends to be easier and cheaper to produce. It can be prepared off-site and transported in refrigerated vans by caterers and therefore can still be supplied even if kitchen facilities are limited. Having a buffet also reduces the amount of waitressing staff needed. However, the food can be prepared to look fantastic and colourful with centre pieces such as dressed salmon or carved cold meats.

- If you decide on a sit-down, three-course meal for your reception, consider altering the menu to a starter, main course and serve your wedding cake for dessert. If the starter and the main course are substantial enough, your guests will not miss a separate dessert and those with a sweet tooth will still have cake and it could save you money.

- Both the barbecue and finger buffet options tend to be cheaper than formal sit-down meals or fork buffets. If you time your reception for early evening and choose these catering options, it could work out more economical than having a formal sit-down reception during the day followed by an evening reception.

- If you choose a venue such as a restaurant or hotel, ask for the various menu options available and check if choosing a set menu or food that is in season can work out more cost effective.

- If you are looking for something a little different to a traditional English reception, perhaps you might want to consider other international cuisines as an alternative (although this will depend upon your location in the UK as to how feasible this is).

Catering

- If using in-house or external caterers is still too expensive, another alternative would be to ask family or friends to help with making food (or perhaps use the concept that each guest should bring a dish). If you are considering a cold finger buffet, it may be possible for family/friends to make trays of sandwiches and other cold buffet food. However, if this option seems to work for you, you will need to consider the following.

    - Numbers of guests and how much food needs to be supplied.

    - Will friends/family have time to make the food and attend the wedding?

    - How will the food be transported to the venue?

    - What the conditions for food preparation and storage will be. Professional caterers have to adhere to food hygiene regulations by law to avoid causing illness. Anyone providing food for your guests needs to be confident they can do this too.

    - Will the venue allow you to choose this option?

4 Wedding Cake

The choice of wedding cake is something personal to the bride and groom, but in recent times choices have become more varied. Couples can now opt for sponge or chocolate cake instead of the traditional fruit cake. I have also noticed that some couples are beginning to alter traditions by not having a cake at all, but replacing it with a chocolate fountain or an alternative centre-piece.

Wedding cake designs are becoming more lavish and intricate and unfortunately prices are rising to the point where even the cake can cost several hundreds of pounds.

(?) Questions for the bride and groom

What type of cake would you prefer?	Fruit cake	☐
	Sponge cake	☐
	Chocolate cake	☐
	Mixed layers to give a choice	☐
	Other	☐
How many tiers would you like?	One tier	☐
	Two tier	☐
	Three tier	☐
What other decoration are you looking for?	Bride and groom	☐
	Decorative piping	☐
	Sugar flowers	☐
	Artificial flowers	☐
	Real flowers	☐
	Other	☐

Why the expense?

It may be difficult to understand why a cake made up of flour, eggs, sugar and raisins can end up costing several hundreds of pounds. However, there is considerable skill involved in icing a cake, as well as the number of hours involved in creating one of the show pieces and focal points of your wedding day.

The more elaborate the design, the higher the price.

In addition, the person making the cake is responsible for keeping it safe during the creation phase, mending any mistakes or problems as they arise (e.g. cracked icing), transporting the cake safely to the venue and also assembling the cake at the venue.

(!) Cost cutting tips and ideas

There are a number of ways to reduce the amount spent on a wedding cake whilst still providing an attractive focal point for your photographs.

Some of the options I have come across recently include the following

- Many supermarkets now supply basic iced fruit and sponge cakes in various sizes. It is also possible to buy pillars so the layers can be assembled into a tiered cake. The packaging often gives ideas on suitable decorations to add to the top of the cake. However, if you are using a florist for your flowers, it may be possible to ask them to produce a floral cake top to keep the theme the same. (The florist will need to ensure any flowers/foliage coming into contact with the cake have not been treated with any harmful chemicals/pesticides that could be transferred to the cake.)

  Prices vary between supermarkets so it is worth shopping around. In my experience, it is not always the most expensive cakes that taste the best. This option also gives you the advantage of buying the smallest sized cake layer in advance so you can taste the cake beforehand.

  In addition to the official display cake, most supermarkets will also sell rectangular iced cutting cakes. These can be sponge or fruit cake. This gives you the option of having a smaller wedding cake but still being able to supply enough cake, for all your guests as well as offering them a choice of fruit or sponge cake.

- As an alternative to the above, there are some internet based companies through which you can order basic iced cakes as well as decorations. If you decide on this route, it is advisable to order sample products in advance to make sure you receive what you are expecting.

- Do you have a relative who would be able to make a cake for you? This could cut the cost considerably or may even be offered as a wedding present. But make absolutely sure they are confident to do the job and will not let you down.

- If you are looking for something less traditional, another option is to create a cake made up of tiers of cupcakes on a suitable cake stand. Some companies specialise in hand crafted cupcakes with sugar flowers on top. Although these are stunning they can cost in the region of £5 each. However, supermarkets can stock iced cupcakes at various times of the year with a variety of designs such as flowers on them made out of sugar paste. It is worth having a look to see what is being supplied.

- A variation of this theme which would be suitable for a winter wedding is a tiered display of mince pies. If these are dusted with icing sugar and decorated with sprigs of holly and other seasonal foliage, this could make a very attractive alternative to a traditional cake.

You will need to work out how many pieces of cake you need for your guests and also to send out to people who are unable to attend the wedding.

Wedding Cake

It is difficult to say how many servings a cake will provide, but if you are buying a cake from a supermarket there should be guidelines on numbers of portions with the cake.

If you are asking someone to make the cake for you, you will need to consult with them on the size to ensure you can get enough portions for all your guests.

The actual number of portions will obviously depend on the size of the slices and how the cake is cut. You also need to remember that if you have a sponge cake and a fruit cake of the same size, you will get approximately two slices of sponge cake for every three slices of fruit cake. For example, if a fruit cake produced 15 slices, you would get about ten slices from a sponge cake of the same size.

You will also need to check in advance whether your reception venue will provide a cake knife or whether you should arrange for this.

5 Car and Chauffeur

Now that the bigger issues of the venue and catering are covered, we can move onto the smaller individual items that are needed to make your wedding day run smoothly.

The bride is usually going to need to have transport from where she is getting ready to where the ceremony is taking place. The bride and groom then need to be taken from the wedding ceremony to the reception.

However, in my experience, the mode of transport can range from a mini-bus (with all the guests) to a friend's car, or to a hire car complete with chauffeur.

(?) Questions for the bride and groom

Is the type of car you have very important to you?	Yes ☐	No ☐	
What type of car are you looking for?	Rolls Royce ☐	Limousine ☐	Vintage ☐
	Other ☐	_____	
Which trips does the car need to make?	1.		
	2.		
	3.		
Do you need transport for the bridesmaids?	Yes ☐	No ☐	

Why the expense?

The (often) short trip from the bride's house to the wedding ceremony and then to the reception will probably work out at an extortionate rate per mile.

However, looking at it from the car owner's point of view, they need to insure and maintain the car all year round.

Again, peak demand tends to be on Saturdays during the summer, and often the car and chauffeur can only be booked for one customer per day, as there is always a risk of over-running. Therefore there is only a limited amount of business a car can be used for.

(?) Questions for the chauffeur

What type of car(s) do you have? _____

Can we come and see the car(s)? Yes ☐   No ☐

Can you take the bridesmaids first and then come back for the bride? Yes ☐   No ☐

What is the price for hiring the car for the journeys we require? £_____

Do you charge extra if the timetable for the day over-runs? Yes ☐   No ☐

If yes, how much extra? £_____

Do you book more than one wedding per car per day? Yes ☐   No ☐

What contingency plans do you have in place if something goes wrong beyond your control? _____

(!) **Cost cutting tips and ideas**

So what can you do to save money?

It all depends on how far you are prepared to compromise with the type of car, but having spoken to many brides and attended many weddings here are some ideas that could work out cheaper for you.

- Vintage cars tend to be more expensive than modern cars, so unless this is one of things you have dreamed of to make you wedding day complete, it should be possible to find a cheaper solution.

- Do you have a family member or a friend with a car that could be used or could they hire a car for the day? (Check insurance cover if considering this option.)

- If you are able to arrange your wedding ceremony and your reception at the same location, you could eliminate the need for a car altogether.

- Is there anyone who could give the bridesmaids a lift, cutting out the need for a second car?

- Or can the chauffeur take the bridesmaids first and then come back to pick up the bride? This would save the cost of having two cars, but does depend on the distances that have to be travelled to ensure it can be done in time.

6 Photographer

Photography at your wedding is probably one of the most important items, as you are going to want to capture the memories of your wedding day.

In my experience there are a variety of ways that photographers charge for their time and for the photos they produce.

Some will charge a fee for their time on the day, with an additional fee if they are required at the reception. They then charge a price per photograph so you can choose as many photographs as you wish.

Others will charge a package price which includes their time and a certain number of photographs. The more expensive the package, the more photographs they will supply.

(?) Questions for the bride and groom

Are the photographs of your wedding very important to you?   Yes ☐   No ☐

Where do you want the photographer to take photographs?

At the bride's house ☐

Before the wedding ceremony ☐

During the ceremony ☐

After the ceremony ☐

At the reception ☐

Have you checked with the registrar/vicar if it is acceptable for photographs to be taken during the ceremony?   Yes ☐

Have you checked with the reception venue if it is acceptable for photographs to be taken?   Yes ☐

Upon speaking to or meeting the photographer, do you feel comfortable with him/her taking your photograph?

Yes ☐   No ☐

Why the expense?

Wedding photographers have acquired their skill over many years. As well as the actual photography, they also need to be able to organise the guests into appropriate groups and so people management skills are also very important.

A lot of responsibility lies with the wedding photographer to get it right as once the moment has passed, it is not going to be possible to recapture it.

In addition, as with chauffeuring, the wedding photographer is only likely to be able to book one wedding per day. As mentioned before, peak times for weddings tend to be on Saturdays during the summer so there is only a limited number of days the wedding photographer can cover.

(?) Questions for the photographer

Do you belong to any professional photography associations?

Yes ☐   No ☐

What is the charging structure for the photography?

_____

How long will you be
taking photographs for?   _____

What type and how
many group photos will
you take?   _____

Do you supply:

  prints   Yes ☐   No ☐

  CD of photos   Yes ☐   No ☐

  photos displayed on   Yes ☐   No ☐
  website

  negatives?   Yes ☐   No ☐

Are these included in the   _____
price or are these priced
separately?

How much are reprints?   _____

Do you have any former   _____
clients we can contact
for a reference?

Can we come and see   Yes ☐   No ☐
you at work at a
wedding?

Can we see examples of Yes ☐   No ☐
other weddings you
have taken photographs
at?

Are you willing to come
and see the wedding
ceremony
venue/reception venue
beforehand?

Yes ☐   No ☐

What contingency plans
do you have in place if
something goes wrong
beyond your control?

_____

(!) Cost cutting tips and ideas

Wedding photography is one of the most difficult areas to save money as
there is usually so much importance attached to wedding photographs.

Here are a few ideas on how to get the best deal.

● Start searching for your wedding photographer very early.
Wedding photographers get booked up many months in
advance and if your wedding is only a couple of months away
you are very unlikely to be able to negotiate a better price for
your photography package. Ask all your family members,
friends and colleagues to see if anyone can recommend a good
photographer from their own experiences of any weddings they
may have attended recently.

● It may be possible for you to choose a basic photography
package with your photographer for a lower price which con-
tains the main photographs you require for the day. You could
then supplement this by asking a friend or a member of the
family to take more pictures at the same time so you end up

with a mixture of 'official' and 'unofficial' photographs. Make sure this person is reliable and confident or ask a couple of people to take on this role.

● Search for photographers/photographic companies who do not necessarily specialise in wedding photography. You may be able to find a photographer who makes a living doing other types of photography during the week, but might be willing to photograph your wedding as a one off.

● There are some companies that offer a wedding photography service where you pay per hour for the photographer's time. The photographs are then displayed on the company website so that you and your guests can choose which images you want to buy and download.

● Whether you choose to have an official photographer or not, a good way to get lots of photographs is to put out disposable cameras on tables for your guests to take pictures. If you attach a label to each camera with instructions asking guests to use up the film and telling them where to leave the camera at the end of the reception, you can send these off for developing and are likely to get a very varied set of photographs. It is also a good idea to give out verbal reminders about the cameras throughout the reception so that people do not forget to use them. You will also need to let people know where to leave the cameras at the end of the night.

● If your photographer charges for their time and for the photograph prints separately, ask him/her whether they can supply gift vouchers. You could then include these on your gift list if you decide to have one.

7 Invitations

Having covered the venue, food, transport and photography, you also need to consider how you are going to let your guests know they are invited.

With some hand-made invitations retailing from £2.50 to £3.75 each, the cost of the invitations alone could amount to several hundred pounds and that doesn't even include the postage!

(?) Questions for the bride and groom

How many invitations will you need?
(Remember to allow for a few handwriting mistakes)

Day time reception _____

Evening reception _____

What style of invitation would you like?

Hand-made ☐
Printed/personalised ☐
Pre-printed/shop bought ☐
Other ☐

Do you want to create your own wording inside the invitation?

Yes ☐   No ☐

Do you want to adapt the wording inside a pre-printed/shop bought invitation?

Yes ☐   No ☐

What colour scheme would you like for your invitations?

_____

What type of design would you like for your invitations?

_____

Have the following
details which need to be
included been organised:

date of wedding	Yes ☐		No ☐
place of marriage	Yes ☐		No ☐
time of marriage	Yes ☐		No ☐
venue for day reception	Yes ☐		No ☐
time for day reception	Yes ☐		No ☐
venue for evening reception	Yes ☐		No ☐
time for evening reception?	Yes ☐		No ☐

Why the expense?

Hand-made invitations tend to be more expensive than other options as they are individually made and therefore the price reflects the materials used as well as the time taken to make them.

Invitations that are printed specifically for the bride and groom also tend to be a more expensive option as the printer will need to create the design and produce only a short print run. However, with new developments in printing technology, smaller print runs tend to be cheaper now than in the past.

 Questions for the printer

If you do decide to have your invitations printed for you, here are some of the things you may want to consider asking the printer.

Can you print:

invitations	Yes ☐	No ☐
order of service	Yes ☐	No ☐
name cards	Yes ☐	No ☐
menu cards	Yes ☐	No ☐
thank you cards	Yes ☐	No ☐
other _____?	Yes ☐	No ☐

Can you show us a selection of designs? Yes ☐ No ☐

Can you show us a mock-up of what the invitation will look like? Yes ☐ No ☐

Is there a minimum order quantity? Yes ☐ _____ No ☐

What is the price for the order? £_____

If we need an additional print run, is this possible? Yes ☐ No ☐

At what cost? £_____

How long will the print run take? _____

Is delivery included in the price? Yes ☐ No ☐ £_____

(!) Cost cutting tips and ideas

Remember that once your guests know about the wedding and have attended, most of the invitations will end up in the bin so is it really worth spending a lot of money on them?

By using a little creativity it is possible to find a solution that looks great but will not cost a fortune.

When researching the wedding industry for my business I found that it was quite easy to find ideas for simple but elegant cards. Here are a few tips to point you in the right direction.

- If you are interested in hand-made invitations, find a design that you like and then copy it. Supplies of card, paper, ribbon, glitter and other accessories can be bought from most craft paper shops. The shops local to me also offer advice or short classes on craft techniques, making it possible for you to create the invitations yourself. Using a PC, it is also possible to create and print your own wording for the inside of the card.

- If you don't have the time or inclination to make your own hand-crafted cards, perhaps you can design something suitable on the PC and print it. Look around for ideas in magazines and in craft paper shops. Creating something simple can still look very elegant and effective. For example, your invitation can be typed and printed on cream paper, but if you add a small amount of confetti into the envelope, the wedding theme will still be set when the invitation arrives.

- Standard design invitations are available at many stationery and card shops. These are usually sold in packets of ten or 15 and will have standard text inside with blank spaces to fill in appropriate details. This is likely to be a cheaper option compared to hand-made or printed invitations, but has the draw-back of being mass produced and therefore not unique for your wedding.

● More recently, with advances in technology, another option is to send out invitations by email which saves on printing costs. However, you would need to decide whether this option would work for you and your guests as some people still do not have access to email.

Other things you may want to include with your invitations

As well as the design and the important information such as the date and time of your wedding and wedding reception, there are a number of other pieces of information you may want to include with your invitation.

Gift list

Deciding whether or not to have a gift list is a very personal choice for each bride and groom. However, if you are considering this, it will need to be organised before you send out your invitations. If you decide against a gift list and do not want guests to pay for presents, it may be a good idea to include 'no gifts please' on the invitations.

Menu options

If your catering option requires guests to choose what they would like to eat beforehand, you will need to include this with the invitation, to avoid having to call all your guests up. It may be possible for you or the caterer to create a simple reply form to make it easy for your guests to respond.

Dietary requirements

Even if your guests do not need to pre-order food, it is a good idea to ask guests to inform you of any allergies or food requirements they may have. If you pass this information on to your caterers, it will enable them to make necessary arrangements to cater for your guests' dietary requirements whilst at the same time reducing the risk of any claims against you or the caterers.

Directions/maps

If many of your guests are travelling from out-of-town, it may be useful for you to provide them with some directions for the wedding ceremony venue and the reception venue. Alternatively, you could mention on your invitation that if they require directions, to contact you.

Accommodation

If many of your guests are travelling from out-of-town, you could help them by supplying contact details of local hotels or guest houses that are near (or at) the reception venue. An idea of price per night would also be helpful.

Programme

Wedding invitations are notoriously vague when it comes to the programme for the day and when guests can expect to eat. It may be useful to consider including some information with the invitation so guests know what will be happening during the day and also what type of food (finger buffet or three-course dinner) will be served and when.

When deciding upon your invitations, you may also need to think about your order of service and thank you cards for after your wedding. If you think about these at the outset, you can ensure they are designed in the same way as your invitations to carry on the theme you are going to set.

Sample Text for Invitations

Below are a few suggestions on possible text to be included in your invitations. However, it is up to you to decide how you prefer the text to be set out and what you would like the invitation to say. If your family circumstances do not conform to the suggestions below, the internet is a good source of information for alternative suggestions on how best to draft your invitations.

Suggestion for invitation to day and evening reception

Mr and Mrs James Jones
request the pleasure of your company
(or: request the honour of your presence)
at the marriage of their daughter

Louise
to
Mr Neil Wood

at
St Mary's Church, Littletown
on Saturday 6th August 200x
at 2pm

and afterwards at their reception at
The Castle Hotel, Littletown
Evening reception and buffet to follow from 7pm onwards

RSVP
1, Main Street
Littletown
LT3 5XX

Please reply by 15th April 200x

Alternative suggestion (for example for older couples)

John Smith and Jayne Price
request the pleasure of the company of

_____

at their marriage at
Hampshire Place, 63 London Road, Middletown, MD3 4BX
on Saturday, 23rd July 200x
at 3 pm

and afterwards at their sit-down reception at the same venue.
Evening reception and buffet to follow from 7pm onwards

RSVP
John Smith and Jayne Price
15 High Street
Middletown, MD4 7GH
Tel: xxxxx xxx xxx

Please reply by 30th April 200x

Suggestion for evening reception invitation (with invite to wedding ceremony)

Mr and Mrs James Jones
request the pleasure of the company of

_____

at the marriage of their daughter

Louise
to
Mr Neil Wood

at
St Mary's Church, Littletown
on Saturday 6th August 200x
at 2pm

You are requested to return later to attend
the evening wedding reception and buffet
at

The Castle Hotel, Littletown

on Saturday 6th August 200x
from 7pm onwards

RSVP
1 Main Street
Littletown
LT3 5XX

Please reply by 15th April 200x

Suggestion for evening reception invitation

Mr and Mrs James Jones
request the pleasure of the company of

_____

at the evening wedding reception and buffet
to celebrate the marriage of their daughter

Louise
to
Mr Neil Wood

at
The Castle Hotel, Littletown

on Saturday 6th August 200x
from 7pm onwards

RSVP
1 Main Street
Littletown
LT3 5XX

Please reply by 15th April 200x

When you are ready to send out your invitations you will save a lot of time if you prepare a checklist of all the names of guests you have invited. You can then tick who is coming and who is not as soon as you get the reply back. This will also make it easier for you to follow up any guests who haven't responded to you by the 'reply by' date.

8 Decorations

The theme set by your invitations can carry on to the theme set by the decorations you choose to have at your reception.

This area is easy to overlook if you get engrossed in all the other items you are trying to organise.

The scope for decorations is very wide as decorations can range from a few small table decorations to drapes on walls, seat covers, large floral arrangements and balloon displays.

However, it is possible to make a visual impact without spending a fortune.

⟨?⟩ Questions for the bride and groom

What colour scheme
have you decided on for
your decorations?

_____

Does the colour scheme   Yes ☐   No ☐
go with the decor of the
venue?

Which of the following
items would you want at
your reception:

   confetti on tables   ☐

   wedding favours   ☐

   name cards   ☐

   menus   ☐

   coloured   ☐
   napkins/serviettes

   ribbons on   ☐
   napkins/serviettes

   centre piece   ☐

   flowers   ☐

   balloons   ☐

   candles   ☐

   draped fabric?   ☐

Why the expense?

As with all the other areas of reception, there is always a price involved if you are paying someone to do a job for you.

Although there may not seem much involved in decorating your venue, you need to keep in mind that if you ask a professional to do the job they have to come up with the ideas, will spend time working out prices, will source materials and create the decorations and then have to travel to the venue and spend time decorating it.

 # Cost cutting tips and ideas

It is possible to save money by making the decorations yourself. You will need to remember to find a volunteer you can trust to decorate the venue for you on the day, as you will be busy preparing for your wedding ceremony.

Some options which I have found to be very successful at wedding receptions I have been involved in organising include the following.

Confetti for tables

Although confetti is not the most expensive item to buy, you need to consider what will go with your colour scheme and you may also want to think about how you can carry on the theme of your invitations through to your decorations to give a totally coordinated look to your wedding.

There are different options for confetti such as metallic hearts or stars, tissue paper hearts or dried rose petals (although these tend to be a more expensive option). Confetti scattered on tables is a very cost effective way to decorate. If you have included some in your invitations, the theme will be set from the start.

Wedding favours

Wedding favours have become a popular way to give your guests a souvenir of your wedding day. Each guest receives a few sugared almonds (or sweets or chocolates)*. These can come wrapped in cellophane or netting and tied with a ribbon, or they could be presented in a small decorative box. It is also possible to attach a label with the name of the bride and groom and the date of the wedding.

Wedding favours are hand-made and can cost in the region of £1.50 to £2.50 each to buy. Therefore supplying these for 100 guests could add another £150 to £250 to your total bill. They can be made at home for a fraction of the price and the design can be co-ordinated with the design of your invitations and other decorations.

The internet is a good place to source chocolates/sweets for your favours, which you can buy in bulk to help keep costs low.

Name cards, menus and seating plan

It may be possible for you to ask the caterer/venue to supply name cards, menu cards and a seating plan as part of the food package.

Alternatively, if you are producing hand-made invitations or designing an invitation on your PC, it may be a good idea to consider name cards, menus and your seating plan at this stage. When buying materials for your invitations, if you purchase the materials for these items at the same time, you may be able to negotiate a discount with the supplier.

If designing items on your PC, you will need to consider how you are going to produce name cards, etc. Stationery shops can supply clear see-through labels so it is easy to type up the names of your guests and print them off. The labels can then be stuck on whatever name cards you decided to have and as they are see-through they do not affect the design of the card.

* See note regarding dietary requirements and allergies in the invitations section.

Table centre piece/flowers/balloons

You may decide that you would like to have a focal point at the centre of your table. There are many options for this so it is advisable to set a budget per table and work backwards to see what you can afford. Here are a few ideas.

Flowers

Flowers are dealt with as a separate subject in this guidebook (see next chapter). Having a floral arrangement on every table could work out quite expensive so an alternative could be to opt for a single flower (such as a rose or a gerbera) in a long vase. If you are ordering bouquets from a florist they may be willing to lend you some vases for the day or you may be able to find inexpensive vases in discount stores or by looking around in the sales.

Glass bowl centrepiece

Another option is to have a glass bowl at the centre of each table. You could fill these with water and have floating candles in them (check regarding fire regulations at the venue). Or you could fill the bowl with novelty items for your guests such as bubbles, party poppers, disposable cameras and sweets. Again, it may be possible to find inexpensive bowls in discount stores or during the sales.

Balloon cluster

Having a cluster of balloons in the centre of the table can look very pretty and helps to give the room a lift. The balloons are usually tied with coloured ribbon to a decorative weight. Many card and gift shops now supply small helium canisters for sale which usually contain enough helium for about 25–30 balloons. However, it is worth checking with a professional balloon company regarding prices, as you may find that by the time you have sourced balloons, ribbon, helium and a volunteer to create the balloon clusters for you it would be more cost effective to pay the professionals.

Candles/tea lights

Some venues will not allow candles/tea lights due to fire regulations/risks. (Battery operated tealights are now available.) However, for the venues that do allow them, candles/tea lights in holders are a great way to add a magical feel for your evening reception. The key is to use a large number of tea lights. Subject to the agreement of the venue manager, tea lights in holders can be distributed on tables, around the finger buffet table and on any flat surface where there is no risk of burning anything.

It is possible to buy inexpensive tea light holders from most home wear shops, however, a friend of mine came up with an alternative of using empty baby food jars which are just as effective.

If it is possible to dim the lights at the reception venue in the evening, the tea lights will provide an atmospheric glow that is bound to be enjoyed by your guests.

Always beware of fire risks and take into account unexpected behaviour of guests and children.

Draped fabric

Another thing to consider is using fabric to add some colour to your reception. Organza can be used on top of white table linen to introduce your colour scheme. Netting can be tied into bows on chair backs. Organza can be pinned into drapes around the top table (or on the front of a stage if the function room has one) and bows can be tied at the top of each drape. (Take into account fire risks mentioned previously.)

Although using fabric will add extra expense, it is possible to source cheaper fabric in a number of ways. Some shops sell fabric seconds at a greatly reduced rate. Any imperfections can be hidden within the drapes or just cut out of the fabric. If you are buying fabric in bulk, it is worth asking for a discount.

9 Flowers

Flowers can be a very effective way of creating a visual impact at your wedding, but it is quite easy for the bill to mount up to hundreds if not thousands of pounds.

There are so many options for flower arrangements including bouquets, baskets for the flower girl, buttonholes, corsages, pew ends, pedestal displays in the church, pedestal displays in the reception venue, table centre-pieces, top table arrangement and buffet table arrangements.

This list could go on further and doesn't even include 'thank you' bouquets that are presented after the speeches.

? Questions for the bride and groom

What colour scheme have you decided
on for your flowers?   _____

What type of flower would you like to
have as the main flower in your displays?

   rose   ☐

   gerbera   ☐

   lily   ☐

   other   ☐

   would like advice from florist?   ☐

Which of the following items are
essential for your wedding day:

   bridal bouquet   ☐

   bridesmaid bouquet   ☐ Quantity _____

   flowergirl basket   ☐ Quantity _____

   haircomb   ☐ Quantity _____

   hair circlet   ☐ Quantity _____

   buttonhole   ☐ Quantity _____

   corsage   ☐ Quantity _____

   pew ends   ☐ Quantity _____

   pedestal arrangements   ☐ Quantity _____

   top table arrangement   ☐

   buffet table arrangement   ☐ Quantity _____

   table centre-piece   ☐ Quantity _____

   gift bouquets?   ☐ Quantity _____

Which of the following items are
desirable (but not essential) for your
wedding day:

bridal bouquet ☐

bridesmaid bouquet ☐ Quantity _____

flowergirl basket ☐ Quantity _____

haircomb ☐ Quantity _____

hair circlet ☐ Quantity _____

buttonhole ☐ Quantity _____

corsage ☐ Quantity _____

pew ends ☐ Quantity _____

pedestal arrangements ☐ Quantity _____

top table arrangement ☐

buffet table arrangement ☐ Quantity _____

table centre-piece ☐ Quantity _____

gift bouquets? ☐ Quantity _____

Why the expense?

Flowers for your wedding can appear expensive, but when you under-stand more about the role the florist has to play in creating your arrangements, it is easier to see where the cost comes from.

The florist has to spend time with you discussing your requirements to gain an understanding of what you are looking for as well as the budget you have in mind. They then have to use their imagination to create a design that will be to your taste and will also fit in with your ideas.

The flowers need to be ordered in the correct quantities to arrive at the right time so they are in full bloom on the right day (and have not gone past their best). The flowers need to be conditioned and stored so that they do not wilt. This is particularly important in hot summer months.

The florist will then only be able to prepare the arrangements the day before the wedding which often involves working late in the night to get everything done.

Finally, the flowers will need to be delivered at the various locations where they are required (bride's house, church, reception venue).

(!) Cost cutting tips and ideas

By considering carefully how you use flowers at your wedding reception it is possible to reduce the amount you spend without compromising the overall visual impact for your guests or for the photographs.

- Consult your florist to see which flowers would be in season on your wedding day and see if these would be cheaper.

- Ask your florist about floral arrangement designs that incorporate a few stunning flowers surrounded by green foliage. Foliage tends to be a lot cheaper than the flowers.

- A hand-tied bouquet tends to be cheaper than a shower or trailing bouquet.

- If you are having pew ends at the church, consider alternating floral arrangements with ribbons so that you need fewer floral arrangements.

- At the reception consider having a single flower in a vase as a centre-piece rather than an arrangement. Or as described in the decorations section, replace flowers with an alternative centre-piece.

Flowers

If you decide on the number and types of arrangements you require and how much money you can afford to spend, your florist will then try to work out a design that will be achievable within that budget.

Take a fabric sample from the bridesmaid's dresses with you to the florist as this will help them to choose appropriate flowers. Also, give the florist details of how tall each bridesmaid is, as this will help to decide on the design of the bouquets, etc.

Once the florist has given you the first quote, it may be possible for you to reduce the price by asking about alternative possibilities such as using different flowers, reducing the size of your arrangements, etc.

You will also need to check that price includes delivery and give delivery times for each location, e.g. bride's house, church/civil ceremony location, reception. Provide a contact name or number for each location so the florist has someone they can call if there is a problem, e.g. they have difficulty finding the place.

10 DJ and Disco/Entertainment

Another area for consideration is how you are going to entertain your guests once they have eaten and all the formalities of the day are out of the way.

Having a disco or live music for the evening reception is a popular choice and gives the opportunity for the bride and groom to have their first dance.

Some people also opt for music during the day reception and arrange for a string quartet or a harpist to provide background music during a drinks reception or while people eat.

(?) Questions for the bride and groom

What sort of music do you require at the wedding service?
(Check with the venue that the music you would like is allowable.)

☐ Solo singer
☐ Choir
☐ Harpist
☐ String quartet
☐ Organist
☐ Other
☐ None

Do you require background music:

during the drinks reception   Yes ☐   No ☐

during the sit-down reception?   Yes ☐   No ☐

If yes, what type of music?

☐ Harpist
☐ String quartet
☐ Other

What type of entertainment would you like for the evening reception?

☐ DJ/disco
☐ Live band
☐ Other

DJ and Disco/Entertainment

Do you want to have:

a first dance   Yes ☐
                       Song title/artist:

_____

a last dance   Yes ☐
                       Song title/artist:

_____

What type/style of music would you   _____
like at your evening reception:

How would you like the
entertainment to be structured during
the evening reception:

break for buffet   Yes ☐   No ☐
background music only during   Yes ☐   No ☐
early evening?

Why the expense?

Although it is possible to find reasonably priced discos, live music tends to be more expensive.

In particular, if you are wanting to hire a group such as a string quartet or a band, once you split the fee between members you will probably find they don't earn a huge fee for each engagement.

The fee they earn also needs to reflect the time they need to put into practise as well as upkeep and transport of equipment/musical instruments.

81

? Questions for the entertainer

What is the charging structure
for the entertainment?   _____

If we want you to play for longer   Yes ☐   No ☐
on the day, are you willing to do
this?

If so, what would be the extra   _____
fee for this?

Can we come and see you at   Yes ☐   No ☐
play/sing at a function?

What type of music do you   _____
sing/play?

Can you accommodate our   Yes ☐   No ☐
special requests?

Requests: _____

Will you require breaks?   Yes ☐   No ☐

If so, how long?   _____

Will you require   Yes ☐   No ☐
food/refreshments?

For the DJ/Entertainers using electrical equipment: is your equipment PAT (portable appliance tested) on a yearly basis?

Yes ☐   No ☐

Can we see a copy of your PAT certificate?

Yes ☐   No ☐

Do you bring back-up equipment with you?

Yes ☐   No ☐

(!) Cost cutting tips and ideas

Music can play a very important role in setting the right ambience and atmosphere at your wedding and reception. If you choose the music carefully along with the visual impact of your decorations, you can create unforgettable memories for your guests.

However, if you are hoping to have music at the wedding ceremony, day reception as well as in the evening, the bill could come to hundreds, if not thousands of pounds, so it is important to make your selection carefully.

- If you require background music at the wedding ceremony or for a drinks reception, consider replacing live music with a CD. You will need to ask for permission to use music during your ceremony if you are having a church wedding, to ensure the person conducting the service is happy with the selection. Register offices do not tend to allow music, however, if you are having a civil ceremony in a hotel, again music may be allowed but you need to make enquiries about this beforehand to ensure it is permissible.

- If you are getting married in a church and would like a choir or soloist to sing, check to see if there is anyone associated with the church already. It may be possible to negotiate a reasonable fee.

- Do you have any friends who either DJ part time or who belong to a band? Again, you are far more likely to have their services for a reduced fee or for free (as a wedding gift). However, you must be certain of their reliability and ability to take this on.

Always inform the venue of the type of entertainment you are hoping to have and any requirements the performer may have (e.g. electric sockets for equipment) to ensure what you are proposing to do is allowable at the venue and complies with all licensing and insurance regulations.

11 Wedding Dress and Other Clothing

And finally, once everything else has been considered, you need to decide what to wear.

Not only do you need to sort our your own outfits, but you also need to consider what the best man and ushers will wear as well as the maid of honour, bridesmaids, flower girls and page boys.

Furthermore, you may want the bride's and groom's fathers to co-ordinate their clothing and you need to check that the bride's and groom's mothers do not end up wearing identical or clashing outfits!

? Questions for the bride

What type of dress would you like?	Traditional	☐
	Modern	☐
Would you prefer:	Two piece (bodice and skirt)	☐
	Dress	☐
What neckline would you like?	Strapless	☐
	Sweet heart	☐
	Scoop round	☐
	Halter neck	☐
	V neckline	☐
	Off shoulder – V neckline	☐
	Other	☐
What type of sleeves would you like?	Sleeveless	☐
	Straps	☐
	Cap/short sleeves	☐
	Long sleeves	☐
	Other	☐

Wedding Dress and Other Clothing

What type of skirt would you like?

Straight ☐

A line ☐

Fishtail ☐

Ball gown/ full skirt ☐

Skirt length: _____

What sort of train would you like?

None ☐

Short ☐

Medium ☐

Long ☐

What colour dress would you like?

White ☐

Ivory ☐

Cream ☐

Other _____ ☐

Is there additional detail you would like?

Beading ☐

Embroidery ☐

Sequins ☐

Lace ☐

Other ☐

Is there a particular fabric you would like your dress to be made of?

Silk ☐

Satin ☐

Organza ☐

Chiffon ☐

Tulle ☐

Other ☐

What other accessories are you planning to wear with the dress?	Tiara	☐
	Veil	☐
(NB it is important to consult your hairdresser about hairstyles available for you with the accessories you wish to wear.)	Jewellery _____	☐

This checklist can also be used as a basis for deciding on the brides-maids' outfits.

? Questions for the groom

Would you prefer:	Nehru jacket	☐
	Frock coat	☐
	Morning tail coat	☐
	Dinner jacket	☐
	Highland wear	☐
	Other	☐
What colour suit would you like?	Black	☐
	Grey	☐
	Cream	☐
	White	☐
	Other	☐

What accessories will you require?	Waistcoat	☐
	Handkerchief	☐
(NB It is a good idea to tie in the colour scheme of these with the colour scheme being used for bridesmaids' dresses, flowers, etc.)	Cravat/tie	☐
	Top hat	☐
	Other	☐

This checklist can also be used for the best man, bride's/groom's father and ushers. However, the groom should stand out and look different from the rest of the wedding party, e.g. by wearing a different tie or waistcoat.

(!) Cost cutting tips and ideas

For the bride

- Wait for the sales in wedding dress shops to try and pick up a bargain.

- Look in chain/high street stores or supermarkets as many now offer ranges of bridal wear.

- Check the small ads in your local paper for a second-hand dress.

- Check auction websites to look for a second-hand dress. (But take care as the photo provided on the site and the final product may look very different.) Check the item description, read the feedback comments about the seller and ask the seller any questions you have before bidding.

- Research the types of fabric that suit the style of dress you like. The type of fabric you choose could have a big impact on the overall price of your dress.

- Carefully consider the style of dress you would like. If you choose a style that requires a lot of fabric, e.g. a dress with a long train or a full skirt, the price will increase.

- Consider selling your dress after the wedding to recover some of the cost.

- Consider simple designs without embroidery. Machine work instead of hand beading can greatly reduce costs. A simple dress with simple accessories can look very stylish.

- Asking a local dressmaker to copy a style of dress in a cutting edge magazine could help save hundreds (and even thousands) of pounds.

For the bridesmaids

- Many chain stores now supply inexpensive dresses for younger bridesmaids.

- Consider looking for older bridesmaids' dresses in the evening wear section of department stores.

- Look for bridesmaids' dresses in the sales in wedding dress shops.

- If you are able to find a dressmaker to make your wedding dress, ask about making the bridesmaids' dresses too.

For the groom/best man/ushers/bride's and groom's fathers

- It is usually cheaper to hire suits than to buy.

- Hire stores may offer a discount if you hire a number of suits from them, e.g four suits for the price of three.

- Alternatively, if you pay for the suit hire, the hire store may hire the accessories for a discounted rate.

Bride's Essential Bag for the Wedding Day

As the bride you will not be able to have a handbag with you, therefore it is advisable to prepare a bag of essential items which you can give to a trusted friend/member of your family you have nearby all day. So, if you need any of the essential items in it, you can still get access to them reasonably easily.

I am sure you can think of all the things you might require, but as a starting point, here are some suggested items you may need:

- make-up — including waterproof mascara
- tissues
- tights
- headache tablets (and any other medication you may require)
- tampons/sanitary towels
- small amount of money
- house key
- toothbrush/toothpaste
- deodorant/perfume
- hairbrush
- mirror
- phone numbers of suppliers and family members
- spare underwear
- _____
- _____
- _____

12 Task List for Planning Your Wedding Day

To do:

- Check information on legal marriage by going to your local council website
- Check information on changing your name on your passport – www.passport.gov
- Open a wedding bank account
- Set a budget for your wedding
- Decide on how you are going to finance your wedding
- Set a wedding date, or preferred time of the year – even if provisional
- Let close family members and friends know the provisional date
- Compile bride & groom invitation list with both families
- Start contacting suppliers for brochures/price lists e.g. chauffeurs,
- Start looking for information on reception venues
- Choose which venues meet your requirements
- Call reception venues and book appointments to view
- Visit reception venues
- Provisionally book reception venue
- Do not confirm until ceremony is booked
- If required, search for caterer for venue
- Arrange wedding insurance
- Choose location of ceremony
- Book the church, registry office, synagogue or licensed venue.
- Personnel at church will advise you on legal requirements etc
- If you are provisionally booking a reception, make a note in your task list to confirm the booking three see
- Provisionally book a date for the wedding otherwise, if you are getting married in a church
- Inform all main people required at rehearsal of date
- Once date of ceremony is confirmed, confirm the reception venue booking
- Pay deposit for reception venue
- Discuss menu options with the venue/ caterer
- Book catering
- Book your hotel for first night
- Search for a photographer
- Meet with a few photographers to look at photographs etc
- Decide what type of photograph package will suit you best
- Check the estimated cost of photographer
- Book photographer for the day

The following is a task list to help you plan your wedding day and to help you think about all the things you will need to arrange.

The timescale is intended to be a guideline only. It will depend on the size of your wedding reception and how complicated your arrangements are as to how far in advance you will need to plan.

If you follow some of the advice on saving money in the guidebook, you may also find that some of these tasks no longer apply as either you or your friends and family are going to arrange something yourselves and therefore you no longer need a supplier to do it for you.

The list may also need additional items adding to it, depending upon what you decide to book.

12–18 months before your wedding day

	Tick ✓
Check information on legal marriage by going to your local council website	
Check information on changing your name on your passport	
Open a wedding bank account	
Set a budget for your wedding	
Decide on how you are going to finance your wedding	
Set a wedding date, or preferred time of the year – even if provisional	
Let close family members and friends know the provisional date	
Compile bride and groom invitation list with both families	
Start contacting suppliers for brochures/price lists, e.g. chauffeurs, wedding cake, photographers, etc	
Start looking for information on reception venues	
Choose which venues meet your requirements	
Call reception venues and book appointments to view	
Visit reception venues	
Provisionally book reception venue (do not confirm until ceremony is booked)	
If required, search for caterer for venue	
Arrange wedding insurance	

10–12 months before your wedding day

	Tick ✓
Choose location of ceremony	
Book the church, register office, synagogue or licensed venue. Personnel dealing with the booking will advise you on legal requirements, etc	
If you are provisionally booking a registrar, make a note in your task list to confirm the booking three months prior to the wedding day	
Provisionally book a date for the wedding rehearsal, if you are getting married in a church	
Inform all main people required at rehearsal of date	
Once date of ceremony is confirmed, confirm the reception venue booking	
Pay deposit for reception venue	
Discuss menu options with the venue/caterer	
Book catering	
Book your leave from work	
Search for a photographer	
Meet with a few photographers to look at photographs, etc	
Decide what type of photograph package will suit you best	
Check the selected photographer is free	
Book photographer for the day	

8–10 months before your wedding day

	Tick ✓
Nominate two witnesses	
Discuss honeymoon plans	
Make sure your passports will still be valid up to the date you're due to return	
Book your honeymoon	
Choose your best man, ushers, bridesmaids/page boys	
Think about wedding dress styles (look at magazines, go and try dresses on)	
Decide on final design of dress and where you are getting dress from	
Order dress	
Think about bridesmaids' dresses	
Decide on final design of bridesmaids' dresses and where you are getting them from	
Order bridesmaids' dresses	
Find beautician and hairdresser you trust	
Consult with beautician and hairdresser regarding your dress style	
Book for trial one month before wedding day and also for wedding day	
Select a gift list	
Sift through/collect information on wedding cars	
Get quotes from several wedding car companies	
Meet with a couple of wedding car companies	
Decide on type of car	
Book car for the wedding day	
Look at cake design options	
Get quotes for cakes	
Decide on place to get cake from	
Place the order for the cake	
Decide if you are having a videographer	
Collect information on videographer	
Get quotes on videographer	
Meet with a few videographers	
Book the videographer you have selected	

Task List for Planning Your Wedding Day

6–8 months before your wedding day

	Tick ✓
Decide on type of entertainment you would like	
Contact a few entertainment providers to collect information and prices	
Find out facilities for music at the venue e.g. loud speakers	
Inform ceremony venue/reception venue of your plans for entertainment to ensure it is allowable	
Select music for wedding ceremony and check it is allowable	
Book entertainment	
Collect some ideas for different wedding invitations and other items, e.g. name cards, order of service	
Obtain quotes for invitations/work out costs for producing them yourself	
Decide on design of invitations and other items, e.g. name cards, order of service	
Decide on wording inside your invitations and the other information you want to include	
Order invitations/make invitations and other items, e.g. name cards, order of service, menus	
Arrange date to collect the invitations from the printers or arrange for them to be sent to you	
Find out if staff at the venue can decorate it for you, or if you can do it yourself	
Look at different designs in magazines for flowers	
Book appointment with florist to discuss type of flowers	
Agree on flowers and book with florist	
Consider your honeymoon requirements, vaccinations, visas, insurance	
Select men's formal wear if hiring formal menswear, choose your preferred style and book the sizes you'll need	
Choose and order your wedding rings	
Contact venue/caterers/photographer/chauffeur/videographer to make sure all is ok with your bookings	

5 months before your wedding day

Arrange for dress fitting	
Buy wedding day lingerie	
Finalise guest list	
Arrange accommodation for your wedding night	

4 months before your wedding day

Fill in invitations and send them to your guests	
Consult with mothers regarding their outfits	
Organise your hen/stag nights	

3 months before your wedding day

List acceptances and refusals to invitations as they arrive	
Choose wedding accessories, shoes	
Discuss your ceremony requirements with your vicar or priest, decide upon church bells, a choir, church flowers, confetti	
Confirm booking with registrar and ensure all formalities/paperwork are in order	
Have you sorted out all the legal requirements for the wedding?	
Check with main people that they are still available for wedding rehearsal	
Take another look at your passport – check everything is in order	
Look at changing your name/address on your bank account, credit cards, drivers licence, social security and utilities – seek advice from these organisations on when and how this should be done	
Check caterers/venue still booked for correct date	
Order table wine and champagne for the toast (either through venue or through caterers or organise this yourselves if allowed to bring alcohol into venue)	
Check florist still booked for correct date	
Check chauffeur still booked for correct date	
Check photographer still booked for correct date	
Check entertainment still booked for correct date	
Check videographer still booked for correct date	
Check cake is still booked	

2 months before your wedding day

Arrange for fitting of dress	
Arrange for fitting of bridesmaids' dress	
Select bridesmaids' gifts	
Purchase presents for the best man, bridesmaids and ushers	
Meet with the photographer to discuss photographs you want taking	
Decide on type of decorations you want	
Buy decorations (and confirm with friends/family regarding decorating the venue) or book company to decorate venue	
Phone all potential guests who haven't replied	

1 month before your wedding day

Arrange for final fittings of your dress	
Wear wedding shoes around the house to break them in	
Get all your holiday clothes together and buy items you need	
Pack bag of bride's essentials	
Arrange a reception seating plan	
Inform venue/caterers of final numbers and of any special dietary requirements for guests	
Check on dresses, suits, etc. Is everything going to plan?	
Collect your wedding rings	
Write the groom's speech	
Arrange foreign currency/travellers' cheques for your honeymoon	
Write down special vows and readings and give to minister/registrar	
Pay for the food/venue	
Pay for the cake	
Pay for the videographer (this might be after the wedding)	
Pay for the flowers	
Pay for the photographer (this might be after the wedding)	
Enrol help of family/friends to help you decorate venue	
Write names on place cards	
Trial run of hair and make up and confirm booking for wedding day	
Confirm time and date of rehearsal with members of your wedding party	

2 weeks before your wedding day

Hold hen and stag nights	
Start honeymoon packing	
Confirm wedding night hotel	
Flowers – inform florist of number of button holes and arrange to have them delivered directly	
Confirmation with venue/caterers	
Confirmation with florist	
Confirmation with chauffeur	
Confirmation with photographer	
Confirmation with entertainment	
Confirmation with videographer	
Confirmation with any other supplier you have booked	
Book taxi or arrange lift to the hotel after the reception/or to airport	

1 week before your wedding day

Collect foreign currency/travellers' cheques	
Hold wedding rehearsal	
Box up all the decorations and label to take to the venue	
Final confirmation with hair stylist and make-up person	

The last few days leading up to your wedding

Organise for hired clothes to be returned while you are on honeymoon	
Organise to collect the cake	
Collect wedding dress	
Final confirmation with venue/caterers	
Final confirmation with florist	
Final confirmation with chauffeur	
Final confirmation with photographer	
Final confirmation with entertainment	
Final confirmation with videographer	
Final confirmation with any other supplier you have booked	
Final confirmation with friends/family carrying out tasks on wedding day	
Give contact numbers of all suppliers to a trustworthy member of your family/friend who can call them on the day if anything doesn't go to plan	
Give contact number of a trustworthy member of your family/friend to all suppliers so they have a point of contact in case of a problem	

The day before your wedding

Decorate venue	
Pick up outfits if hiring them	
Give rings to the best man	
Give your passports, travel tickets and money to friend or family member	
Speak to all attendants	
Arrange for holiday/going away clothes to be put in the boot of your car or at your first night hotel	
Give your bride's essential bag to friend/family member who will be with you all day	
Relax and have an early night and set your alarm clock	

Budget Planner

In order to keep your spending as low as possible you will need to work out how much you can afford for each part of your wedding reception and stick to that budget or better still, try to spend less.

If you make a detailed list of all the things you require for your wedding reception you can break the budget down, which will make it easier for you to manage your spending.

Here is a list to get you started, but there are spaces to add extra items which you may want to include.

Item	Budget	Actual cost
Invitations		
Postage		
Bride's dress		
Bridesmaids' dresses		
Bride's shoes		
Accessories		
Wedding rings		
Groom's attire		
Best man/ushers' attire		

Church/civil venue		
Order of service		
Reception venue hire		
Catering – day reception		
Catering – evening		
Drinks reception		
Drinks for toast		
Wedding cake		
Entertainment		
Flowers		
Decorations including favours/place cards/menus		
Transport		
Bride to wedding service		
Bridesmaids to wedding service		
Groom to wedding service		
Bride and groom to reception		
Bride and groom away from reception		
Photographer		
Videographer		
Wedding night accommodation for bride/groom		
Honeymoon		
Total		

Liz's final tips for planning your wedding reception

- The earlier you start planning the better. Looking for the best options for your venue, food, car, cake, photographer, DJ, etc will be time consuming and if you leave it late it will put more pressure on you as well as potentially missing out on the best deal.

- Take out wedding insurance at an early stage for cover required.

- Make sure you agree everything with your suppliers *in writing*. If you and the supplier have all the details written down there is less scope for a mistake to be made. Ensure the correct wedding date is written down. Check the services/items to be provided are described clearly and a price is agreed. If there are optional services, make sure these are listed separately and any additional costs for these are clearly defined.

- Always check with each supplier what their back up plan is in case something beyond their control goes wrong.

- If you receive a price list from a supplier that is out of your price range, speak to them to see if they can accommodate your budget and find out what they can provide for that amount of money. The worst thing they can say is 'no', but on the positive side you may be able to persuade them to work to your budget.

- Once you have made a booking, keep checking at regular intervals that everything is in order. Ring around every supplier you have booked with a few days before your wedding for a final check.

So now, having finished reading this book, I am handing planning and organising of your wedding reception over to you.

I hope the checklists provided in this guidebook are useful to you as well as the ideas and tips aimed at saving you money.

Although planning a wedding can be very stressful, it is important to keep in mind that as long as both of you (the bride and groom) arrive at the wedding service and get married, that is all that really matters.

Good luck!

Appendix: Questions

(?) **Questions for the organisers**

	Stag	**Hen**
What is the budget per person for the stag/hen night?	£_____	£_____

What is the location for the stag/hen night?

Stag		Hen	
At home	☐	At home	☐
Local	☐	Local	☐
Other city	☐	Other city	☐
Outside UK	☐	Outside UK	☐

What activities will you want to take part in on the stag/hen night?

Stag		Hen	
Watching football	☐	Spa/beauty	☐
Gokarting	☐	Pub crawl	☐
Paintballing	☐	Meal out	☐
Pub crawl	☐	Nightclub	☐
Meal out	☐	Karaoke	☐
Nightclub	☐	Other	☐
Karaoke	☐	_____	
Other	☐	_____	
		_____	

What are the costs per person?

Activity £_____	Activity £_____
Drinks £_____	Drinks £_____
Food £_____	Food £_____
Nightclub entrance £_____	Nightclub entrance £_____
Transport £_____	Transport £_____
Accommodation £_____	Accommodation £_____
Clothing e.g. printed t-shirts £_____	Clothing e.g. printed t-shirts £_____
Other £_____	Other £_____

⑦ Questions to ask the venue

Can the venue accommodate the number of guests?   Yes ☐   No ☐

Is there a separate room or area to hold the reception away from other customers?   Yes ☐   No ☐

Can the hotel or guest house restaurant area be converted into a private function room?   Yes ☐   No ☐

Can we use the dining area for our reception on the day of the week we are proposing to hold it?   Yes ☐   No ☐

What options are available for food?

Hot sit down waiter service ☐
Hot fork buffet ☐
Cold fork buffet ☐
Finger buffet ☐
Barbecue ☐
Other ☐

Is there a licensed bar available?   Yes ☐   No ☐

What time are last orders? _____

Is it possible to get a bar extension? ☐ No ☐

If yes, is there an extra cost for this? Yes ☐ £_____ No ☐

Is it possible for us to bring wine/sparkling wine/champagne? Yes ☐ No ☐

Is there a corkage fee associated with this?

Wine £_____
Sparkling wine £_____
Champagne £_____

Will the venue supply glasses if we bring our own wine/champagne? Yes ☐ No ☐

Will there be an additional cost for this? Yes ☐ £_____ No ☐

Is the venue child friendly? Yes ☐ No ☐

Are the toilets in good working order? Yes ☐ No ☐

Are there enough? Yes ☐ No ☐

Is there enough parking? Yes ☐ No ☐

Appendix: Questions

Is there accommodation available on site for guests?	Yes ☐	No ☐
If yes, what would be the cost per night?	£_____	
Is it possible to get a discounted rate if the reception is held at the venue?	Yes ☐	No ☐
If no, where is the nearest accommodation for guests?	_____ _____ _____	
Is it possible to have a disco for the evening reception?	Yes ☐	No ☐
Are there any restrictions regarding this such as noise or space?	Yes ☐	No ☐
Is the hall in a suitable condition to hold a wedding reception?	Yes ☐	No ☐
Is the hall suitable and clean enough to serve food?	Yes ☐	No ☐
Is the hall available for hire on the day of the week we are proposing to hold it?	Yes ☐	No ☐

Will the hall provide:

tables	Yes	☐	No	☐
chairs	Yes	☐	No	☐
linen	Yes	☐	No	☐
crockery	Yes	☐	No	☐
cutlery	Yes	☐	No	☐
glasses?	Yes	☐	No	☐

What cooking and cleaning
facilities are available?   _____

_____

_____

Are there any caterers   Yes ☐   No ☐
associated with the hall?

Is there a licensed bar   Yes ☐   No ☐
available?

What time are last orders?   _____

Is it possible to get a bar   Yes ☐   No ☐
extension?

If yes, is there an extra cost Yes ☐ £_____   No ☐
for this?

Is it possible for us to bring Yes ☐   No ☐
wine/sparkling
wine/champagne?

Appendix: Questions

Is there a corkage fee associated with this?	Wine	£_____
	Sparkling wine	£_____
	Champagne	£_____

Will the venue supply glasses if we bring our own wine/champagne?   Yes ☐   No ☐

Will there be an additional cost for this?   Yes ☐   No ☐

Is the venue child friendly?   Yes ☐   No ☐

Will the hall be heated?   Yes ☐   No ☐

Can the hall accommodate the number of guests?   Yes ☐   No ☐

Are the toilets in good working order?   Yes ☐   No ☐

Are there enough?   Yes ☐   No ☐

Is there enough parking?   Yes ☐   No ☐

Is there accommodation available on site for guests?   Yes ☐   No ☐

If yes, what would be the cost per night?   £_____

Is it possible to get a discounted rate if the reception is held at the venue?

Yes ☐   No ☐

If no, where is the nearest accommodation for guests?

_____

_____

_____

When can access be gained to the hall to prepare for the reception?

_____

When does the hall have to be vacated?

_____

Who is responsible for cleaning and tidying the hall?

_____

Will the hall provide staff for:

the bar   Yes ☐   No ☐

the cloakroom   Yes ☐   No ☐

moving tables and furniture?   Yes ☐   No ☐

Is it possible to have a disco for the evening reception?

Yes ☐   No ☐

Are there any restrictions regarding this such as noise?

Yes ☐   No ☐

? Questions for the in-house catering manager

What type of food can you provide?

And at what prices?

Hot sit down waiter service	£_____
Hot fork buffet	£_____
Cold fork buffet	£_____
Finger buffet	£_____
Barbecue	£_____
Other	£_____

Can you give us some menus to show what type of food you can supply?

Yes ☐   No ☐

Are the following items included in the price:

table linen	Yes ☐	No ☐
crockery	Yes ☐	No ☐
cutlery?	Yes ☐	No ☐

Can you supply vegetarian options?

Yes ☐   No ☐

Can you supply separate meals for people with specific dietary requirements?

Yes ☐   No ☐

Is it cheaper to choose a
set menu for my guests?   Yes ☐   No ☐

If we set a budget per
head, can you provide a   Yes ☐   No ☐
menu option for that price?

Is it possible to come and   Yes ☐   No ☐
see a function you are
providing the catering for?

⑦ Questions for the external caterer

What type of food can you provide?	Hot sit down waiter service	£_____
	Hot fork buffet	£_____
And at what prices?	Cold fork buffet	£_____
	Finger buffet	£_____
	Barbecue	£_____
	Other	£_____

Can you give us some menus to show what type of food you can supply?   Yes ☐   No ☐

Are the following items included in the price:

table linen   Yes ☐   No ☐

crockery   Yes ☐   No ☐

cutlery   Yes ☐   No ☐

waitressing staff   Yes ☐   No ☐

staff to clear up?   Yes ☐   No ☐

Can you supply vegetarian options?   Yes ☐   No ☐

Can you supply separate meals for people with specific dietary requirements?   Yes ☐   No ☐

Is it cheaper to choose a set menu for my guests?	Yes ☐	No ☐
If we set a budget per head, can you provide a menu option for that price?	Yes ☐	No ☐
Do you clean up after the function?	Yes ☐	No ☐
Is it possible to come and see a function you are providing the catering for?	Yes ☐	No ☐
Have you catered at this venue before?	Yes ☐	No ☐
Will you be willing to visit the venue with us beforehand to check the facilities are suitable for the type of catering we require?	Yes ☐	No ☐

What is your contingency plan if something goes wrong beyond your control, e.g. van breakdown

 Questions for the chauffeur

What type of car(s) do you have? _____

Can we come and see the car(s)?   Yes ☐   No ☐

Can you take the bridesmaids first and then come back for the bride?   Yes ☐   No ☐

What is the price for hiring the car for the journeys we require?   £_____

Do you charge extra if the timetable for the day over-runs?   Yes ☐   No ☐

If yes, how much extra?   £_____

Do you book more than one wedding per car per day?   Yes ☐   No ☐

What contingency plans do you have in place if something goes wrong beyond your control? _____

? Questions for the photographer

Do you belong to any professional photography associations?

Yes ☐   No ☐

What is the charging structure for the photography?

_____

How long will you be taking photographs for?

_____

What type and how many group photos will you take?

_____

Do you supply:

prints   Yes ☐   No ☐

CD of photos   Yes ☐   No ☐

photos displayed on website   Yes ☐   No ☐

negatives?   Yes ☐   No ☐

Are these included in the price or are these priced separately?

_____

How much are reprints?

_____

Appendix: Questions

Do you have any former
clients we can contact for a
reference?

_____

Can we come and see you
at work at a wedding?

Yes ☐   No ☐

Can we see examples of
other weddings you have
taken photographs at?

Yes ☐   No ☐

Are you willing to come
and see the wedding
ceremony venue/reception
venue beforehand?

Yes ☐   No ☐

What contingency plans do
you have in place if
something goes wrong
beyond your control?

_____

? **Questions for the printer**

Can you print:

invitations	Yes	☐	No	☐
order of service	Yes	☐	No	☐
name cards	Yes	☐	No	☐
menu cards	Yes	☐	No	☐
thank you cards	Yes	☐	No	☐
other _____?	Yes	☐	No	☐

Can you show us a   Yes ☐   No ☐
selection of designs?

Can you show us a mock-   Yes ☐   No ☐
up of what the invitation
will look like?

Is there a minimum order   Yes ☐ _____   No ☐
quantity?

What is the price for the   £_____
order?

If we need an additional   Yes ☐   No ☐
print run, is this possible?

At what cost?   £_____

How long will the print run   _____
take?

Is delivery included in the   Yes ☐   No ☐ £_____
price?

⑦ Questions for the entertainer

What is the charging
structure for the
entertainment?   _____

If we want you to play for   Yes ☐   No ☐
longer on the day, are yu
willing to do this?

If so, what would be the   _____
extra fee for this?

Can we come and see you   Yes ☐   No ☐
at play/sing at a function?

What type of music do you   _____
sing/play?

Can you accommodate our   Yes ☐   No ☐
special requests?

Requests: _____

Will you require breaks?   Yes ☐   No ☐

If so, how long?   _____

Will you require   Yes ☐   No ☐
food/refreshments?

For the DJ/Entertainers using electrical equipment: is your equipment PAT (portable applicance tested) on a yearly basis?   Yes ☐   No ☐

Can we see a copy of your certificate?   Yes ☐   No ☐

Do you bring back-up equipment with you?   Yes ☐   No ☐

Index